I wish I could... SLEEP!

A story about being brave

Tiziana Bendall-Brunello
Illustrated by John Bendall-Brunello

QEB
QEB Publishing

Little Bear was trying to go to sleep when he heard a strange screeching sound.

Little Bear felt a bit scared.

"Oooooh!" he said to himself. "I wonder what that was?"

Little Bear peered around
the edge of the cave.

"Hello, Little Bear!" said Owl.
"What are you doing out here?"

"Well, I heard a scary sound
coming from the tree..."
replied Little Bear.

"That was only ME!" said Owl.

"I wish I could sleep,"
yawned Little Bear.

"Why don't you try my bed?" suggested Owl.

So Little Bear climbed into Owl's nest and tried to get comfortable.

He wriggled a bit.

He turned a bit.

But then...

CRACK!

...Little Bear started to fall.

"Ooohhhh!"
called Little Bear.

Luckily, Little Bear fell right into a big pile of leaves.
"Now I really want to go home to MY bed,"
he sighed.

But he was suddenly startled by something rustling in the leaves beside him. Little Bear froze.

"Hello, Little Bear!" said Raccoon. "What are you doing here?"

"Ahh, it's you," said Little Bear. "I just want to go back to my bed. I wish I could sleep."

"I'm collecting more leaves to make my bed warm and cozy," said Raccoon. "Would you like to try sleeping in my bed?"

"Thank you!" said Little Bear. But try as he might, he could not fit into Raccoon's bed.

"Oooh, I just want to go home," wailed Little Bear.

So off he went...but suddenly he saw a
strange shadow moving across the path.
"Oooooh!" cried Little Bear. "What's that? It looks like a..."

"Hello, Little Bear!" said Moose gently. "Don't be afraid. It's only me. What are you doing out here?"

"I couldn't sleep," said Little Bear. "But now I just want to go back to my bed."

"Jump up here, then—I'll give you a ride!" said Moose.

"When I can't sleep, I just think of something I like," said Moose. "Why don't you try that, Little Bear?"

That's just what Little Bear
did, and In no time at all...
he was fast asleep.

"What a brave Little Bear you are!" whispered Moose softly. "Night, night!"

Notes for parents and teachers

- Look at the front cover of the book together. Ask the children to name the animal. Can the children guess how the animal feels?

- Ask the children what happens at night. Can they see the moon? Can they see any stars? What do they do before they go to bed? Do they wash, brush their teeth, and give their mom or dad a big goodnight kiss? Do they take their teddy bear to bed?

- Can the children name all the animals in the book? Ask them which animal they like the most and why.

- Talk about the leaves, including their size, color, and shape. You could ask the children to collect different sizes of leaves and paste them on a sheet of white paper.

- There are many things that Little Bear is afraid of. Discuss with the children what these are and why. What do you think made Little Bear afraid of the moose? Discuss why Little Bear should not be afraid of a moose, despite the difference in their size.

- Ask the children if they have sleep problems like Little Bear. Discuss what makes people sleep well. Discuss why it is important to have a good night's sleep.

- Ask the children to draw a picture of themselves sleeping, along with all the things that help them sleep well.

Consultant: Cecilia A. Essau
Professor of Developmental
Psychopathology
Director of the Centre for Applied
Research and Assessment in Child and
Adolescent Wellbeing, Roehampton
University, London

Editor: Jane Walker
Designer: Fiona Hajée

Copyright © QEB Publishing, Inc. 2011

Published in the United States by
QEB Publishing, Inc.
3 Wrigley, Suite A
Irvine, CA 92618

www.qed-publishing.co.uk

ISBN 978 1 60992 069 2

Printed in China

Library of Congress Cataloging-in-Publication Data

Bendall-Brunello, Tiziana.
 I Wish I Could SLEEP!: A story about being brave / Tiziana Bendall-
Brunello ; illustrated by John Bendall-Brunello.
    p. cm. -- (I wish I could--)
 Summary: When Little Bear goes into the woods to identify the scary
noise that awakened him, Owl and Raccoon invite him to try out their
beds but Moose finally gets him to sleep and returns him to his own ca
 ISBN 978-1-60992-108-8 (library bound)
 [1. Sleep--Fiction. 2. Bears--Fiction. 3. Forest animals--Fiction.] I. Bendall-
Brunello, John, ill. II. Title. III. Series.

 PZ7.B431352Sle 2012
 [E]--dc22

                                                    2011003288